THE TALE OF DRIED TEARS

Seerat Kaur Munjal

BookLeaf
Publishing

India | USA | UK

Presentation by *BookLeaf Publishing*

Web: www.bookleafpub.com

E-mail: info@bookleafpub.com

ISBN: 9789360945961

First edition 2024

This book is dedicated to my beloved mother,
Late Tajinder Kaur Munjal.

ACKNOWLEDGEMENT

The author lacks words to express her utmost honor to her beloved mother, Late Tajinder Kaur Munjal's heavenly blessings, which became a beacon of hope, light and energy to lift the quill and scribble her emotions with the ink of tears on the reams of life.

She owes a deep sense of gratitude to her late grandfather, Bhupendra Singh Josh Munjal, whose inherited intellectual qualities strengthened her command over literature, which came as a forte in her life.

The author is also thanking from the core of her heart for the constant showers of guidance, love, and blessings from her beloved father, Dr. B S Munjal, her loving sister, Dr. Simrandeep Kaur, and her little niece Arveen Kaur, who were with her in this difficult journey of coping from the loss of a parent to ultimately writing this book as a tribute, as she expresses her beauty of vulnerability and art of conveying her true self through written words.

The author will fail in duty if she forgets to thank the Almighty who gave her strength and will hopefully continue to keep her away from all the evilness of the world...

~ Seerat Kaur Munjal

PREFACE

"Sometimes tears are a sign of unspoken happiness and a smile is a sign of silent pain..."

'The Tale of Dried Tears' is a tribute to her late beloved mother whom she lost on 12th May 2021 in the extremity of the cruel pandemic, which the author brings forth for all the populace of the world who also lost their loved ones in an untimely misfortune.

This book will touch every sensitive cord of the readers who are silently suffering this agony, while their wailing and sobbing tears of misery have now unsparingly dehydrated though they are constantly longing and yearning for the deceased loved one.

The author believes that this treatise collection of her poignant verses will act as a healing and empathetic companion because grieving for a loved one is hard, but healing from it is even harder.

The author believes her contribution will act as an elixir in the hearts of the suffering humanity.

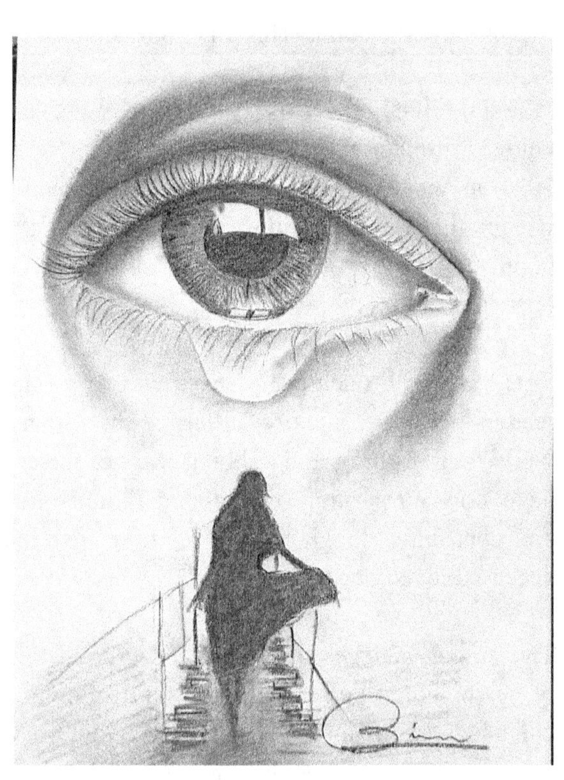

The Tale of Dried Tears

As the umpteen miserable years roll by,
Her absence is like the darkness of the night
sky…

Wandered lost in a maze to chase the stars,
The dimness is so deep and larger than my
scars…

They say death is the most painful feeling of
detachment.
And we must face it without any abandonment…

My heart, so heavy and hard as stone,
The eyes that used to cry have now dried and
lone…

The feeling of her presence in her bedroom,
Her closet, full of her fragrances that gloom…

The delusion of trickery when I use her stuff,
The life after her deceives like a bluff…

Still hope, she's the immortal bird that
regenerates from ashes,
As my withered eyes have dried tears and
forever perish lashes…

Wish to access Heaven

If I had known about my mother's departure,
I could have taken a moment's respite from
God...
Because,
Some words remained unsaid...
Some feelings remained unexpressed...
Some emotions remained unfelt...
Some wishes remained unfulfilled...
Some conversations remained unfinished...
And I wish I could have access to heaven,
As some thoughts remained incomplete
And some promised hugs became a deceit...

Grief feels like

Grief feels like you are screaming and no one can hear you,
Grief feels like the thoughts are piercing like a screw...

Grief feels like I can trade anything for an extra minute with her,
Grief feels like I could substitute everything to make her live forever...

Grief feels like drowning in the deep sea,
Grief feels like I have been locked in a room that has no key...

Grief feels like all my achievements are tinged with heartache,
Grief feels like all the happy moments with her were at stake...

Grief feels like life is merely walking on the egg shell's side,
Grief feels like a part of me was also gone when she died...

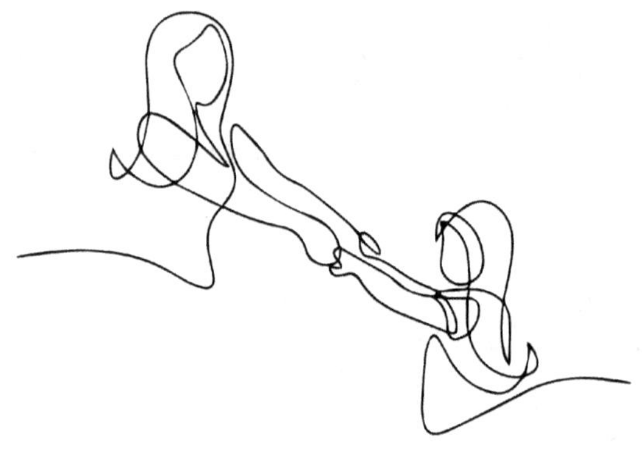

Nobody taught to live without Mother

Nobody taught me to live without a mother,
The very thought suffocates like a smother...

To face the hellish world and all the lies,
Her absence is as if the sun hides behind the
skies...

No one to guide through the night,
No one to wipe away the tears in sight...

No one to soothe hurting hearts,
No one to mend the shattered parts...

No one to show the way in the state of
obscurities,
No one to confront in the fray of duties...

No gentle hand to lead the way,
No one to heal like a ray of the day...

No comforting voice to embrace the pray,
No tender presence that is bound to stay...

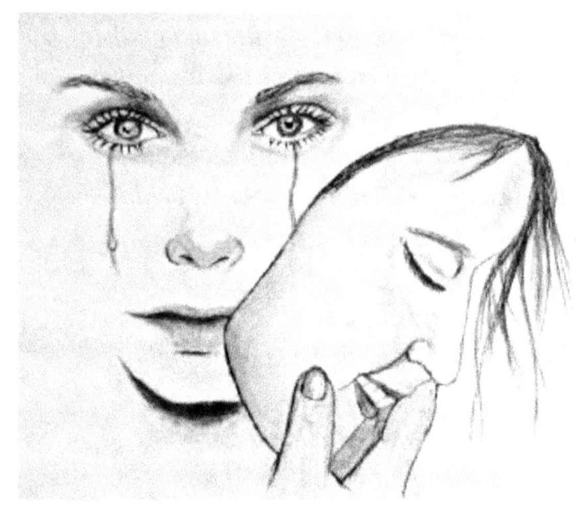

No time to Grieve

In a world full of insensitive lures,
Where love and kindness go in vain and have no
cure…

We are all born with a heart so pure,
But the soul still longs for a love that's hard to
endure…

The flowers that once bloomed are now fade,
The beauty of love is nothing but a mere shade…

For in the world, love's lost its way,
As kindness is far distant and has nothing to
stay…

The streets filled with empty hollow sounds,
Echoes of evilness are so profound…

The world does not even allow time to grieve,
What they say is to, 'move on,' and hide your
pain under the sleeve…

Thought that I'd be able to live for a while,
Because it's easier to hide the pain under a
smile…

Endless sorrow

A heavy burden weighs upon my heart,
An endless sorrow forever lingers as a soul had
to depart...

A muted and subdued hue glitched on a spun,
An aching soul felt the loss of a loved one...

The emptiness and silence, where once there was
light,
Now, blackness that surrounds and damages like
a blight...

The tears I've shed, the sighs felt in pain,
Reminiscence of her presence is now tainted
with disdain...

The grief has no bounds to end,
It's like a burden that made my veins twirl and
bend...

In the depths of sorrow, her memories remain,
As to me, now the rest of the world feels like a
mundane...

Silent Pain

Within life's serene silence,
Lies the pain of unsaid poignance…

Creating a symphony of verses,
That remained as deep dark curses…

When agony lit large on the countenance,
Even the shadow left being our acquaintance…

Nobody mustered the courage to decipher the truth,
Forced to accept the reality as if it was smooth…

Enchanting the powerfully pleasing remembrance,
Restricting emotions and temperance…

Scattered along the fragrance of memories,
Enticing relief of sigh-like breezes…

Reliving the moments which were bound to glean,
As she had created a life which remained unseen…

Profound Emptiness

In discreet instances, your truancies are intense,
Your presence and your smile in my life were
immense...

Days gone, emptiness profound,
Keeping your memories bound...

Maa, I Wish you were here by my side,
Leading the way to be my guide...

My rovering eyes try to find you.
In every virtue, through every view...

With each day passing by, my heart shatters,
The realization is all that matters...

Somehow, I have accepted the fact,
To live with your memories is the only tact...

Yearning to meet you in another life,
The only hope that allows me to be alive...

Agonic Waves

Agony comes in ferocious waves,
Memories make us slaves...

Sorrow comes in ripples,
As volatile as it fickles...

Reminiscence rides on tide,
Precarious it is to glide,
Which tends to submerge and hide...

Anguish over the loss of yesteryear,
Emphasizing it with every burning tear...

Crippling affliction causes harm,
Heartbroken while losing every charm...

Sufferings in life cause misery,
Where the souls elate is still a mystery...

Pain of melancholy sores distress,
Torturing every core, making a mess...

Currents of torment, streams breach border,
Memoir of bereavement making it wider...

Submerging into the vast expands of the sea,
Which one may, never ever again see..

Motherly Love

Distance lends enchantment to ears,
That state of being under a spell feels like
years...

When death's bitter fleet seems supreme,
Flashbacks of memories stare like a beam...

A strong bond held me close even through miles,
Reminiscence of endless gestures in every
smile...

My mother's love shines through the realms of
the sky,
Whispering everlasting boundless notions
behind every sigh...

On the wings of my dreams, I'll cherish every
moment passed,
Motherly love lives eternally surpassing every
hurdle at last...

Tears of the soul

Tears of the soul, a symphony of grace,
A consonance of sorrow, that rolls off the face...

Death is the echo of our deepest fear,
A refrain of hope, a hymn that steers...

Though they bring relief, but leave behind a
stain,
A reminder of how hurt we are, through a
burden to sustain...

Its beauty is the reflection of the pain within,
That we fail to recall when we were
overwhelmed up to the brim...

In the depths of sadness, we prevail over the
hurdle called death,
A resilience that will forever prolong our life's
strength...

Rust of Memory

My soul is entwined with rust,
As if the agony is stuck in the gut…

Flashbacks of the moments spent with her,
Somehow now feels like a blur…

I'm separated from her due to destiny's game,
Trying to live this life again…

Emotions are sometimes sublime,
Passing through each corridor of time…

Showering unconditional love from the heaven
above,
My mother pushed all my ordeals with the act of
shove…

Through the cycle of grief, faith reverberates,
Fabricating roads of hope in our fate…

Her habits shall remain deep in my heart,
Living with her memories is the only art…

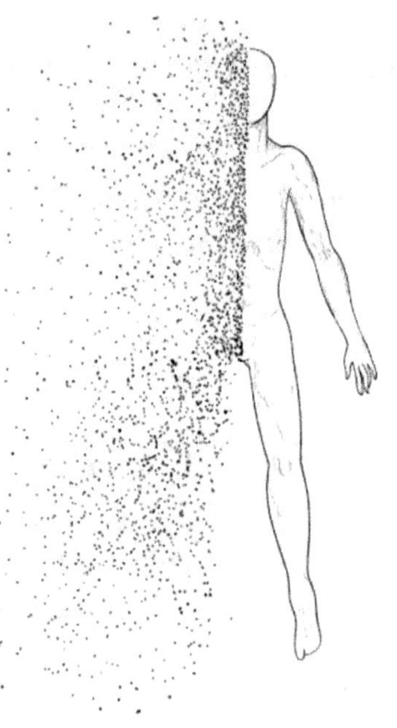

Dust on the Soul

Soul when gathers the dust,
Umpteen evils surround the crust…

As it fosters the insanity and lust,
Divine purging of the dust becomes a must…

Soul wanders across the cosmos,
Without gathering any moss…

Colossal precious moments are flowing like a
gust,
Gathering the thick dark layer of rust…

Rare opportunity to attain salvation is lost,
The only solution is to remember the Almighty at
any cost…

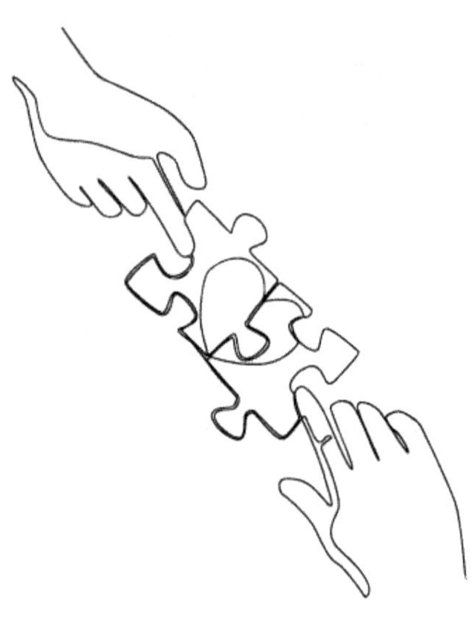

Mosaic of Yesteryears

Hidden in the mosaic of yesteryears,
Mom's nonexistence with her dears...

Her warmth, the narratives she used to gyrate,
Now, only symphonies are left with us that
resonate...

The echoes of her laughter reverberate striking
the roof,
The home once, now looks like a spoof...

The void created pierces our hearts,
Despite trying to live, we are unable to restart...

Her whispers lingered like a dew on a leaf,
Daily reminds us of the pain of grief...

We are lost in the meander of what once was
true,
Now, again trying to live, without any clue...

The hope that happiness will again show up
Because the agony has created an envelope...

Sure to meet her in another life
As life without her stabs like a knife...

Shadows of Memories

In the silhouettes cast by the dusky sky,
Her memories, once vibrant, are now dry...

Fathoming the affection that has stayed,
A mother's love is now lost in a cascade...

Remembering her in every situation with much
despair,
Cursing the universe in every affair...

Nothing helps in overcoming a great loss,
Our happiness unintentionally mislaid in a
toss...

Though unearthing the fact inch by inch,
Cannot accept and react every time with a
flinch...

Camouflaged always in a gloomy stench,
My mother's absence is a dry thirst which can
never quench...

Startled responses and stress became a hobby,
What it's like to be emotionally saturated and
sobby...

Now, life looks like a falsehood and deception,
Hope to meet her in the next birth is the only
perception...

Today

Today, I met a mother who had lost her child,
The emotions we exchanged were priceless and
mild...

With us mutually comprehending that we faced a
loss,
By embracing her, I felt like our life went on a
toss...

The proliferation of agony when someone is lost,
We both hugged each other with welled eyes as
we were tired and frost...

Words lacking, lips shattering, with a sign of
deny,
Neither could she utter a word nor did I dare to
reply...

The amount of pain we could feel was visible,
The inability to show the suffering was even
more miserable

If

If blessings be bestowed,
If the bodies did not corrode…

If heartbeats could synchronize,
If we were all born wise…

If we could love an entire universe,
If we did not fall for any curse…

If the stars could align,
If we could all age fine like wine…

If only our hearts would disperse,
If we could roam around every traverse…

If we could unapologetically love all our scars,
If we could wholeheartedly accept what's not in our stars…

If we could feel the whispers of forthcoming enchantments,
If we could accept ourselves without any enhancements…

If the cosmos guides us to make our dreams a reality,
If we could all stay away from the rule of mortality…

Read between the lines

Some do not understand the circumstances,
Some are unable to decipher the nuances...

Different is the depth of every individual,
Like the Almighty cannot be unearthed in
rituals...

Some can fathom the blank pages,
And some are unable to grasp the heap of
scripted pages...

Seen are the humans without any attire,
Located also are attires on bodies blurting
satires...

Cruel Truth of Life

Death leaves no one apart,
Even if you have love in your heart...

As soon as a person goes, never comes back,
The rules of the Almighty are hard to crack...

Cherish every memory known,
Don't let them fade away from your own...

Anger and greed come in way as hurdle,
Tearing apart and making us dull...

But life can turn things round,
As death spares no one around...

Lest I forget

It's a tale of love and loss,
A memory that even time cannot erase across...

Even if all woods of the Earth make my pen,
And all waters of oceans fill my inkwell's glen...

Even if all surfaces of grass converge as a
canvas sight,
The words would never be enough, that I write...

The ink may flow like rivers toward the sea,
But it cannot express the longing in me...

Lest I forget, the memories of love, loss, life, and
death,
All woven together in a tapestry of breath...

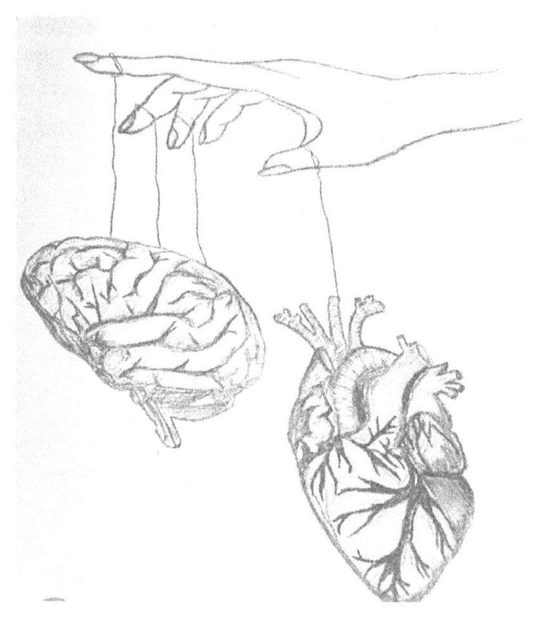

Quest of Mind

From time immemorial of our existence,
A quest is hidden as a timeless persistence...

Beneath the subtle hope where time takes its
stand,
Narratives of the universe are written on its
unfolded hand...

Humans wander in the meander of doubt,
Searching for their worth throughout...

Desirable is the harmonic personage,
Gazing the intertwined destiny on a pilgrimage...

For the ultimate goal of our birth is salvation,
Resonating sync with God's every creation...

Forever a quest will linger on our minds,
As the life lived was worthwhile or just
dissipated in the grind...

Ink of Tears

*Withered are the petals of rose that are lost in
bare pages,*
*Immortal are the feathers that became the
symbol of love for ages*

*Alluring is the tail that forms the quill to imprint
the plain verso,*
*Unfinished is the work of art that defines the
formidable torso*

Ink flows through the brush's stroke with grace,
*A stream of emotions that its beauty cannot
replace*

A melody of love, a treasure that keepsakes,
*Words are wrapped in the arms of a vellum that
forever remains forsake*

*Unending verses certainly conceal the
bereavement that yearns,*
*Because no matter how you decorate the tomb,
the deceased one never returns...*

Melting Moon

*Moon that shines bright with forever secrets
untold,
That the death of a beloved is hard to unwind
and a treasure to behold*

*Moon melts, even the heaven weeps for the soul
that wings,
Cry the welled eyes, even the stars chorally sing*

*Crescent shape marking hope through the
ethereal silver light,
Moon, a reminder of the life's fleeting might*

*Illuminates the night, leaves behind a trail of
dreams,
As Moon melts into the morning dew, forming a
subdued gleam*

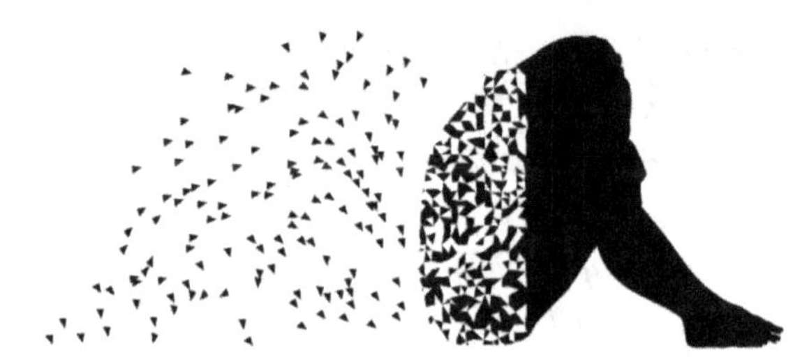

Withered Loss

*The twisted, dark, withered heart that once
bloomed,
Breaches uncountable cracks that are carved
and fumed*

*The petals that once weaved a rhythmic sway,
They now perish and fade throughout the day*

*The curled, intricate, and dark heart,
That was once full of life, is now torn apart*

*A decayed love lost in an endless dismay,
Their demise, a void that whispers loss in an
ethereal pray*

*Though seasons pass and time slowly tries to
heal,
But the pain of bereaved loss is what it can
never conceal*

Fate cheats

Fate cheats, as her inevitable demise feels like a lie,
My eyes, so dry that they cannot even cry ...

Uncertain is the dauntless gamble that takes on,
That suddenly a person moving around is
forever gone ...

A harsh certainty that's extremely hard to accept,
Even after myriad tears that were uncontrollably wept...

People presume that it's insane to still remember and mourn,
Silly ones who fail to fathom that our lives are still indelibly torn...

With a heart of stone, the universe engulfs a soul,
Creating gaps in our hearts like a hole...

Lost Souls

Invisible colourless souls are intricately lost,
And who doesn't rebound back at any cost...

No hue, no shade, yet so profound,
Their presence felt, though unseen, is all
around...

The souls thaw and barges of emotions unleash,
As their heartbeats are discontinued to infinitely
cease...

Leaves behind a rigging depth of bruised pain,
That an elixir of patience starts flowing through
our veins....

Their voice, once audible, now whispers in
space,
Their presence, once so sure, now but a mere
trace...

Their love, light, and laughter once bloomed,
now appear as a haze,
Their hearts are eternally locked which now feel
like a daze...

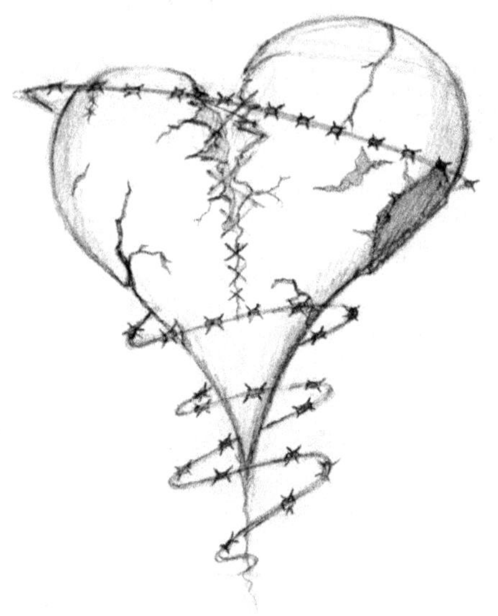

Blemishes of Loss

Fate casts imprints of painted scars on the frail heart,
Leaving behind the traces forming a delicate art

Weaves fathomlessly an intricate drapery,
Blemishes of loss etched into the folds like a treasury

A canvas of heart tinted with the brushes of time,
Bears streaks of every moment on the frail of mind's shrine

Feeble are the walls of such hearts, so pure,
Fragile are the veins that had to suffer through misery to endure

Grief carved each curve, the story of sorrow that was told,
Distress scratches on the tale of life, that has now grown old

In the depths of such hearts, every part tells a story,
A testament to the human spirit, eternally diminishing its glory

Tired Hearts

*The hearts when tired will find embrace on every
ream,
Penning every story of the soul that resonates
with the dream*

*The tears dry in between every metaphor,
Smiles lost within the repetitive galore*

*Preserving hope amidst the rhyme of life,
Altering every emotion that conceals to disguise*

*Dead emotions breathe within the verses of
grief,
Ripping apart the heart of patience in every
belief*

*The wounds are covered over the years under
the skin of a smile,
Where the piece of their presence is lost at the
bottom of the pile*

*On the surface of the ink, the scars bleed,
To just have a glance of the departed one, is the
only greed*

Unfulfilled Wish

*The fleecy seed of a dandelion that flies towards
the sky,
Each gliding desire that forms upon our sigh...*

*Millions of our wishes that were basking in the
pavilion,
Starring hard on the flying seeds of the
dandelion*

*Hereby, cursing our ordeals while gliding
towards the oblivion,
Trying to wash our hardships and misfortune
across the alluvion*

*Whispering a wish, hoping the destiny would
believe,
What if the deceased one could ever return on a
breathless eve...*

*Thawing the walls of the sun-tanned scars,
What if we could change what's written in our
stars...*

The Grieving Grief

Even when the grief grieves,
Trees shed their autumn tears in the form of
leaves

Even the light in the sky before the sunrise fades,
As the umpteen miserable years of togetherness
are in gloomy shades

Even with the holy breeze of cosmos zephyr's
despair,
To survive hard even through a day feels like a
dare

Even when the grief grieves,
A persisting sorrow that won't leave

A burden that we can't ease,
A pain that we cannot retrieve

A melancholic longing of the past that yearns to
remain,
The tears we thought we had cried still linger to
sustain

The outside world seems to be a place of laughter and glee,
Our memories of joy now prick like an unexplained plea

A heart that lost its pride, a soul that lost its light,
A bittersweet world that doesn't seem to be polite

For even when the grief grieves,
We are just left with pain and a burden that we won't be able to relieve...

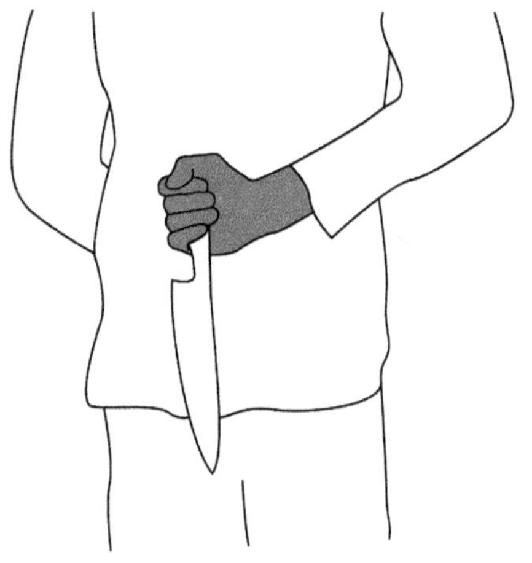

Tactical Shrewdness

Even the kind is accused of selfish and ulterior motives,
As courtesy and decency will forever be considered vilified and furtive…

Even if you give the world, the best you can,
It may still never be enough to satiate the greedy clan…

Even the cruel states hoax tears while the saddest smiles the brightest,
As they say, the most damaged people are often the wisest…

Even the deceptive and guileful are admired throughout,
While the virtuous are viewed with scorn and doubt…

Even the selfless deeds are twisted and distorted,
Whereas compassion and generosity are often mocked and assaulted…

*Even the abuse and disparagement are often
praised,
Whereas generosity is seen as weakness and
often slaved...*

*Even the unspoken thoughts are wrapped in the
longing for selfishness,
The irony is, in the world of disdain, what's only
applauded is the tactical shrewdness...*

*Even when the world accuses, mocks, or even
scorns,
The kind will continue to love, care, and
mourn...*